Blue Pearl

NEW DIRECTIONS POETRY PAMPHLETS

Blue Pearl

Lesley Harrison

NEW DIRECTIONS POETRY PAMPHLET #20

ACKNOWLEDGMENTS
"North: Birds," "Blue Pearl," "Bird Song," and "May, Adventfjord" have been published in *Poetry Ireland Review*, *Northwords Now*, *The Dalhousie Review*, and *The Antigonish Review*. With many thanks for their hospitality to Ole and Thrine Gamst-Pedersen, Ilulissat Kunstmuseum, Greenland.

Cover design by Erik Carter
Interior design by Eileen Baumgartner and Erik Rieselbach
Manufactured in the United States of America
New Directions Books are printed on acid-free paper
First published as New Directions Poetry Pamphlet #20 in 2017

Library of Congress Cataloging-in-Publication Data
Names: Harrison, Lesley.
Title: Blue pearl / Lesley Harrison.
Description: New York, NY : New Directions Publishing, 2017. |
Series: New Directions poetry pamphlet
Identifiers: LCCN 2017009772 | ISBN 9780811226837 (a new directions poetry pamphlet : alk. paper)
Classification: LCC PR6058.A68837 A6 2017 | DDC 821/.914—dc23
LC record available at https://lccn.loc.gov/2017009772

10 9 8 7 6 5 4 3 2 1

ndbooks.com

New Directions Books are published for James Laughlin
by New Directions Publishing Corporation
80 Eighth Avenue, New York 10011

Very end of land. What vast is there?

—W. S. Graham, *The White Threshold*

CONTENTS

ANGEL

Clione limacina

like a gas flame
blue to bluing

hermaphrodite, wingfoot
lead white   still born

asleep / sleepless
repeating its

perpetual
bloom and fall

lucent,
thin as radium

in ice black   slow deep
remnant   starveling

MAY

Adventfjord, Svalbard

*

stone waves
grinding at the edges

a brash and slew
a squalor of gulls:

their land voices
make thick marks in the mud.

*

geese arrive, altering the air
a clamour, an exhaling
their shifting wingbeat

their actual voicings
pure word sounds
for grass and meltwater

*

a sanderling,
lacing the tideline

its thin pleep
like ice melting.

*

plover, ptarmigan:
wind birds

whirring and quivering,
scraping a hole

of lichen and willow bud
of insect wing and down,

small love
blanching the ocean.

*

as snow falls,
condensing

from a dull sky
opaque, paper white

as arctic terns
clothe themselves in light

so that rising
they vanish

BALAENA BOREALIS

from *The Naturalist's Library. Vol XXVI. Whales, etc.*
by Robert Hamilton (London, 1861)

More timid than any other order:
the iris white behind the mouth, the spiracles

indented, the lips, the abdomen yellowing with age.
Its surfaces are furrowed, the sinews dividing into threads;

the bones and soft parts unctuous,
the scarf no thicker than a parchment, shrinking when touched.

They are most generally solitary,
hiding in long green streams of arctic water,

vanishing before the slightest breath, discharging
a thin miasma, like smoke, then sinking

back into the abyss, leaving only dark on the surface.
Its membranes are thin and transparent

and line the walls of native huts, like glass;
its lithe ribs arrows, for darting at sea birds.

RUNE POEMS

The text commonly called the Icelandic rune-poem is
only a poem by courtesy.

—R. I. Page, Viking Society for *Northern Research* (1999)

canker   a tumour

a gall

a dog rose

antimony   a brittle, bluish element

the universal versus the particular

the tinting of the eyelids

noctilucent   high pitched

elusive, neither plant nor animal

a thin polar cloud

nacreus   the *dura mater*

shiny, opalescent

like the inside of a shell

border snow, forgetful
the imposition of narrative
a narrow road lined with clouds

knot the foetal heartbeat,
fluttering, indistinct
like a bird over waves

aporia a butterfly, the black-veined white
an open wound
a point of undecidability

ILULISSAT

Outside

outside myself

there is a world,

he rumbled, subject to my incursions

—William Carlos Williams, *Paterson*

i.
impossible.

sterile extrusion
the rigour of its beauty

its crumpled geometry
worked to defeat.

light, stopped.

locked in its form
shuttered and windless

in dry rifts,
split, furrowed, mottled, creased.

ii.
trundling
bulging from behind,

its too heavy body
its natural carapace

shelving green,
sinking the sea beneath it

the difficulty piling up,
rising to the surface.

iii.
swirling backward
on blue flowering currents

rolling up
sudden, in spray and mist

– like the turning of a page
that leaves us blinded for a second –

unlocked in a milky scum
half hid, long on its axis

growing open wounds
of violet, emerald, silver.

a point of astonishment.
lapses of silence. air.

NUDE

from Pia Arke's exhibition *Arctic Hysteria* at Greenland's
National Museum & Archives, Nuuk, 2010

i.

I am in my body. I am here, in front of you. I am the temperature
in this room. I am undressed in my nudity; I am the light and shade
you feel. I am more like other people than like you. I have before
and after. I am my self, entirely and only. My outside and inside are
continuous. I am muscle, organ, fluid, bone. I am monumental. You
are the only one who sees me.

ii.

I am not naked as I am; I am naked as you see me. I am transparent,
almost visible. I have a time and a place. I am tribal and exotic. I must
always carry objects. You are heroic. I am a complete museum, the
story of my own making. I am a mirror to you; you are reflected in
the looking at me. At best, I mimic you. You write me. When you
leave, I will no longer exist.

iii.

I am a single conscious point. I am indifferent. I am unself, like a
photogram. I am prehistoric, before definition. Your body falls over
me. I have depth and luminescence. I am neither here nor there; I
have infinite extension. I live inside the lived world, the light and dark
inside my head like dream substance. I am camera obscura, the room
itself. I both adore and resist.

BLUE PEARL: POEMS FROM ICELAND

REYKJANES

beneath the tarmac
is a gravel shore
a bay of black sand

a hundred white gulls
seeded like pearls
along the sea edge.

close the city door. listen:
and the wind becomes words
worked smooth, like the handle of an axe

a language rough and dry as sticks;
or the moan
from red holes sinking in the turf

bare vowels
that fill the mouth like lichen.

SANDOY

a cult of light
a calm, white sea
a garden behind the wind.

an old man, lean as a hare
plays mouth music to a foal
dancing on a slope

his falcons tethered to the roof;
their clean, brown shins
cut the air like water.

here, long hills lie
like neighbours,
quiet in their houses

blue and black,
the sea slicing pebbles,
the horse kicking time.

GRENSÁS

in a temple of trees
a woman stands in a stream

dragging eels out of the current
the cool air thickening their spines

long lines unfurling,
a lip of water round her ankles

its silver ounces gathered in bowls,
mirrors of light and dark.

EYRI

winter
hunting by quartz light,

low in their furrow
still as stone

each tiny throat
a hole in the wind.

HÆLL

dry light
earth light
ash light
storm light

blue pearl, touching the horizon.

GJOGUR

a farmer is peering at the light.
he catches the rain in his mouth

green rollers curl above his head
the sea exhaling like an old horse

and dogs scutter on the shale,
sliding into waves as the bay tilts

like a ship, straining as it heels,
pulled by a needle pointing north.

BIRD SONG

from Hull's *Scottish Birds* (Mercat Press, 2001)

heather peeper, hoodie craw
apple sheelie on a waa
lum lintie, peedie geg
cleckin on a speckled egg

water waggie, yella tail
water bobbie in a burn
benny ducker, jenny wren
lucky penny for a bairn

lang sandy, lorin, loom
mally, mootie, horra goose
tammy norrie fae the bass
canna kiss a bonnie lass

whaup, wheetie, peesie thrum
heather bleater, myre drum
churr, chackie, blackie hen
croodle doo an coorie in

EDAY, NORTH ISLES

GUITH

> a greylag morning,
> the sea a conscious blue.

CALF SOUND

> orca
> in a sea blue room,
> breathing pearls that rise to the surface.

GROATHA

> the plenum of the shed:
> every part infilled with flutter,
> glass, sheep turd, gusts of damp.

GREENTOFT

> gunshot punctures a field
> of geese, their clackety rise
> a flock of helicopters.

THE SETTER STONE

> an old man steps out of the ground
> all lines and angles,
> suns snagged in his beard.

MILLCROFT

    a tree softened house:
    red willow, alder, pine,
    eucalyptus rooting.

WARNESS

    a stream hole
    a pure, dense fall;
    one ocean falling into another.

PLANTATION

    wren, silver lark, crow
    woody snipe, curlew, hen hawk
    day owl, starling.

SOUTH END

    the *Varagen*, beaded with spotlights
    curves through the dark
    round great holes in the sea

WARD HILL

    climbing with the moon,
    the wind blowing round my mouth –
    a low note, like an owl.

FROM "NATIVE CUSTOMS"

David Hawthorn Cardno, *Journals of Whaling and Sealing Voyages*.
December 31, 1869. University of Aberdeen Manuscripts Collection.

the young ice was made that we could travel
the most prudent course was to bear
this morning, as during the night
these long dense fogs, which made us anxious

her husband all through was kind to her
for two weeks, helpless and starving
an igloo was made, and into it
all that was comfortable was taken out

it is the custom to leave everything
no one may enter the place of the dead
all huts removed from the corpse
she met his view erect, eyes staring

we rolled her in her own skin, a blanket
and buried on the other side, beyond
this dark and outer boundary of earth
and then we returned on board ship.

THE VOYAGES OF WILLIAM BARENTS

from the journals of Gerrit de Veer, 1609, in the exhibition of relics at the Rijksmuseum, Amsterdam, with drawings by Siân Bowen

Let us look into the White Seas:
>   into the seas directly sailed behind Norway,
>   along and about Muscovia:

In the country lying under 80 degrees,
>   there is both leaves and grass,
>   hartes, hindes, and suchlike beasts;

the contrary in Nova Zembla. There groweth neither.
>   For even when we have no night
>   it grows colder as the sun grows nearer;

yet as soon as we made from the land
>   and put more into the sea
>   presently we felt more warmth;

for it is not the nearness of the Pole
>   but the land ice, by reason of its depth
>   and fastness, in long, inclosed valleys

making it far colder here,
>   even tho these places are not yet discovered,
>   than our low countries.

*

at 100 fathom	no ground
at 120 fathom	oasie, and black durt
at 60 fathom	an oasie small sandy ground
at 52 fathom	white sand mixed with black, somewhat oasie
at 40 fathom	grey sand mixed with white
at 38 fathom	a red sand
at 39 fathom	small grey sand, with black stippellen
at 60 fathom	a little black, and great hollow shells

*

a milk glass sky,
like paper windows.

a soft paper sky.

*

At evening, the first ice:
we thinking it a great mass of swan
drifting out toward us

curving like spindles,
their long necks buckled, hanging
as they glide like sleep against the current.

At midnight we sail through them,
sea glass hissing all round us.

*

A bright north glitter;
an island, unfixed.

*

Winding south again, today we found
a great store of sea horse,

short haired, mouthed like a lion
but smoother round the human part. Our men

went ashore, and presently they found one
alone, on a flake of ice, coddling her young

in small tones, pooled in sunlight,
milk blebbing from her gorged teats

while her pups nuzzled, lolling
as we rose to strike. When she turned, roaring

and cast them before her into the water,
plunging with them in her arms

before rearing again and again, stricken and snorting,
revenging herself upon our hull, grinding

her head upon it, breaking all our gear
in pieces, and still we could not kill her;

when the sea grew hollow, and old ice
clashed about our scuts, forcing us to fall off

back inside the wind,
and thus soon we left the ice behind.

*

2pm. A hail storm
rattled the panes.

We stopped,
and went on in sunlight.

*

This island is visible for hours,
a grey light on the horizon.

Behind these desolate sea beaches
all is enchanted ground:

a naboland
of circles and grave mounds

and images
in great abundance

and cabinets of ice and frost
and ice clouds – porcelain, alabaster;

a labyrinth of internet corridors
of blue, constant air –

trivet, map, catholicum
candles, salt, paper.

*

the	cold	gradually augmented
a fresh	cold	gale out of the east
but very	cold	; we went into the land
immediately fell in with the	cold	and the ice. Indeed
fair starlight weather, and the	cold	still increased
yet very	cold	; we caulked our house
the days growing longer, the	cold	began to strengthen
and very	cold	, which put us in great fear
defend ourselves from the	cold	and the wild
with great	cold	, danger and
to see so great a	cold	, and know not what to think

*

like a map left out over winter
its surface and folds exposed

its lines and contours unshading
like old hills filling and rounding

old words silvering in daylight
unprinting – the action of silence

a true north, drawn by erasure
as snow falls   as light is in paper.

*

lacuna   a gap or hiatus
                  a pattern in reflected light
                  an intercellular space

*

Until we saw the coast of Russia lie before us –
we altogether heartless and faint

and rowing nearer, stroke our sails,
the sun to the north, and found

a river spurting clean white water;
high stiff dunes, a thin turf

of larch and silver birch, increasing
woods of young pine, almost lambent, and beech

a grey green tapestry
that lifted and settled for miles, seeded with wind lights

its parched musk, its latent heat
filling our breathing.

The steep sun of the forest.
The absence of the sea.

*

spoonwort   here are my slow leaves
         here is my tongue
         here are my sprouting arms
         here are my white stars

*

And saluted them after their manner
And looked at each other steadfastly;

For that some of them knew us,
Amazed that we had lived so long

We abashed, standing on the shore
Wherewith our hearts became heavy

For many more words we could not use,
Which made us long to be gone.

*

polar campion   a glass bloom
                                    intravenous white,
                                    like milk in water,

                                    as dry as amnesia
                                    conscious, nodding.
                                    an attention to air.

*

From the low land to the Point of Desire	*6 [24] miles*
From the Point of Desire to the Orange Islands	*8 [32] miles*
From the Orange Islands to Cape Comfort	*25 [100] miles*
From Cape Comfort to the black cliffs	*24 [96] miles*
From the black cliffs to the two islands	*28 [104] miles*
From the two islands to the White Sea	*130 [520] miles*

NORTH: BIRDS

SNIPE
It sprouts from the ground, rasping against stones and reeds like dry rain, or wind, or autumn. The soft organs are tucked away in a small pouch near the heart. It lays down growth rings, like a tree.

EIDER
A clean bird, well woven. It finds a hole in the water, and waits, crooning its undersong. A pot of feathers.

GOLDEN PLOVER
A clear wind; a water eye. A warm breath above the ground. A dip of mottled eggs.

SNOWY OWL
Their eyes are beetled. They are lupine, furred. They fly up to the outer air, white fading into white, seeding the clouds with snow.

PTARMIGAN
Their pinions are wind-sharpened. They roost on a sun-warmed stone. In summer they rattle the grass above the tree line. Their young have cowls of lichen.

PURPLE SANDPIPER
A bird that keeps its shadow under its wing. They exist only in the distance, in scrapes and tangles, fluttering dislodged like holes in daylight. The relic of a storm.

IVORY GULL
It is mute, like a pearl. It holds its own dull gleam, like a lamp in winter rooms. It feeds on light alone.

LULLABY

Once there was a woman
who gave birth to a seal
white as haar, furred like a glove.

It slid into the world
in a rush of kelp and brine,
moon-eyed, cold as starlight.

She wrapped it in the sea's green
till it grew warm,
unbending from her

a slow form uncurling
finding pools and holes in the tide,
rocking itself gently under.

Now, she dreams
out on a shallow ledge,
covered in a net of stars

singing to her child
with the slow, full breathing
of the ocean;

and from the hidden edges of the deep,
a brown moan
lulling her to sleep.

THE SNOW QUEEN

A preterist: one who collects cold nests.

—Vladimir Nabokov, *Pale Fire*

Spring   The sun paints the sides of trees
a lead along their joints.

now the seasons roll back;
the ground yields up its bodies.

a raven beats its black wings.
the larch, its mild arthritis.

Gerda   she dances in daylight
a blank sunny surface
as pure as a doll
shoeless, forgetful

the strange old woman   The sun stops at the lintel
where she wavers,

mild and faded
in the rain

her redpoll nest,
her bright blank windows

neat in the
tropics of her garden.

Her eyes glow
like tail lights in the distance.
Come in, my child, come in.

Spitzbergen   A cape
of thin blue mountains;

their northness,
their clarity of silhouette.

the town   But who saw the children disappear?
Who runs for lanterns and torches?
Who feels the jolt of their absence?
Who searches cars at the border?
How smoothly our story continues!
The days fit neatly together,
the year rolls forward to its close.
How easily our grief grows old!
How seamlessly the wound closes over!

the Snow Queen   she vanishes   ascending
vaporous as hoar frost

sterile, bristling
particles of ice light

her spasms of fur
her whole body breathing

as emerald, ichor
fall from her eyes

seed   small icon,
        a thing condensed

        the pithy shell
        the soft adventitia

        rose red
        curled in a velvet hood

        wee incubate
        tight in its bud.

Kai   Poor Kai. Tired by his dreams,
        he woke and found himself asleep

        speeding north in great white darkness
        deeper and deeper through the ice.

        She turns, and draws the boy child towards her,
        lavishing with cold his hair, his wrists, his puny legs.

        He crawls up inside her fur.
        She kisses him into a kind of death.

the Finland woman　She lives
between stone and air
north, with the world behind her

sitting at her borealis stove
milling winds,
the sun loose on its bearings.

Her whale lamp swings
from the ribs of her ceiling.
Outside, the hard blue ocean.

She snaps her fingers, and water boils.

roses　But look – the attention of roses:
their forced heat

their sweet red tongues
their dozen needy heads

their frostburn canker
their bleeding and peeling.

Gerda   All night she wanders
through blue-black corridors

of surfaces and shadows
and brute cold snowdrifts

barefoot, gleaming gently
as fretful winds curl round her.

She cries, and her tears become angels.
Already her footprints have vanished.

the town   Our cars are parked in the street.
The people walk by with umbrellas.
The snow has melted to rain.

The present occurs and occurs
(a simple arrangement of time
when part of the story is missing).

Kai   Night falls   the sky pales
the still, hanging valleys
in clear grey gleam.

far out he sits
ordering and ordering
in parts and small adjustments

a pure clear world
of glass forms, and delicate imaginings
of intervals and silence.

Such is the privacy of dreams.

the Lapland woman   The world is her island
the sky her reflection
the sea her blue blanket.

at night it lifts and settles, lifts and settles.

south   rain.
how we return to our bodies,
the human work of fields

and hedges, labyrinths
of pavement and birdlight.
the natural magic of trees.

true love   homeward, hand in hand
like two sweet birds,
their childhood out of season

the sky
perfect, weatherless.
blue – the colour of nothing.

the ice palace   the corridors sink into shadow
the hills grow wide in the distance
the moon rolls back on its cradle
the small rooms filling with feathers

thaw   a thin melt
like ink melting into water

a gloved sound,
its sleeves and whispers

a trick of air
in high, stony places

a white sound –
absolute, like music.

home Our story comes back to its source:
the seasons regress into Spring
a boy and a girl, unaging

Pinned like insects
in a rose-lined window,
the town spread out like a story

Here and not here,
the way clouds vanish in the mirror.

hawthorn its silence.
its grey threads.

its fixed arms.
its bright, red berries.